BRIGHT
IDEA
BOOKS

BARACK
Obama

by Jenny Benjamin

CAPSTONE PRESS
a capstone imprint

Bright Idea Books are published by Capstone Press
1710 Roe Crest Drive, North Mankato, Minnesota 56003
www.mycapstone.com

Library of Congress Cataloging-in-Publication Data
Names: Benjamin, Jenny, author.
Title: Barack Obama / by Jenny Benjamin.
Description: North Mankato, Minnesota : Bright Idea Books are published by Capstone Press, [2019] | Series: Influential people | Audience: Ages: 9-12. | Audience: Grades: 4 to 6. | Includes webography. | Includes bibliographical references and index.
Identifiers: LCCN 2018036583 | ISBN 9781543557954 (hardcover : alk. paper) | ISBN 9781543558272 (ebook) | ISBN 9781543560404 (paperback)
Subjects: LCSH: Obama, Barack--Juvenile literature. | Presidents--United States--Biography-Juvenile literature.
Classification: LCC E908 .B47 2019 | DDC 973.932092 [B] --dc23
LC record available at https://lccn.loc.gov/2018036583

Editorial Credits
Editor: Claire Vanden Branden
Designer: Becky Daum
Production Specialist: Colleen McLaren

Quote Source
p.4, "Sen. Barack Obama's Victory Speech." *Abcnews.go.com*, November 4, 2008

Photo Credits
Alamy: American Photo Archive, 21; AP Images: Charles Dharapak, cover; Getty Images: Nuccio DiNuzzo/Chicago Tribune/Tribune News Service, 10–11; Newscom: John Gress/Reuters, 13, Michael Kleinfeld/UPI, 16; Rex Features: AP, 26; Shutterstock Images: Africa Studio, 31, Everett Collection, 6, Henryk Sadura, 15, Joseph Sohm, 5, 19, 28, Paolo Bona, 25, Rena Schild, 22–23; Yearbook Library: Seth Poppel, 9

Printed in the United States of America.
PA48

TABLE OF CONTENTS

CHAPTER 1

MAKING
History

"America, we have come so far. We have seen so much. But there is so much more to do." Barack Obama ended his speech. The crowd cheered. Obama had just made history. He was the first African-American to be elected president of the United States.

Barack Obama was elected president of the United States in 2008.

The crowd cheered for Obama and his family after his historic win.

Obama won in November 2008.
He gave his winning speech at Grant
Park. He and his family were in Chicago,
Illinois. They walked onstage. People
shouted, "USA!" Lights flashed.
The crowd waved flags.

Obama became the 44th president
of the United States.

CHAPTER 2

THE GROWING Years

Obama was born on August 4, 1961. His mother was white. His father was black. The family lived in Hawaii. Obama's parents divorced when he was 2 years old.

Obama was a great student. He also enjoyed playing basketball. He went to college in California and New York.

Barack means "one who is blessed" in Swahili.

In 1985 Obama moved to Chicago. He worked for the Developing Communities Project. He helped train people for jobs. He also worked to make life better in government housing.

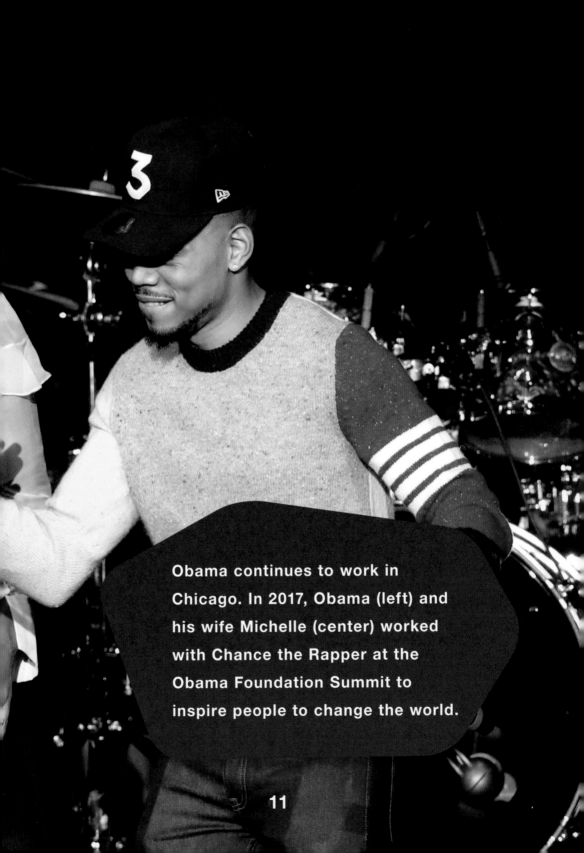

Obama continues to work in Chicago. In 2017, Obama (left) and his wife Michelle (center) worked with Chance the Rapper at the Obama Foundation Summit to inspire people to change the world.

A NEW CHAPTER

In 1988 Obama went to Harvard Law School. There he met Michelle Robinson. They fell in love. They got married in October 1992. They have two daughters. Their names are Malia and Sasha.

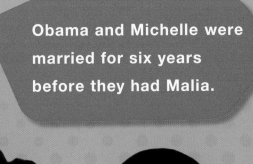

Obama and Michelle were married for six years before they had Malia.

CHAPTER 3

EARLY
Work

Obama wanted to help people. He moved back to Chicago after law school. He taught law classes. He also was the director of Illinois Project Vote. This group worked to get more African-Americans to vote.

Obama became an Illinois **senator** in
1996. He had this job for eight years.
He helped poor children get health care.
He cut taxes.

Obama worked for the
Illinois state senate
in Springfield, Illinois,
from 1997 to 2004.

Obama was sworn in to the United States Senate on January 5, 2005.

Obama ran for the United States Senate in 2004. He won. He became the fifth black senator in history. Obama brought people together. He pushed for lawmakers to be fair. He worked to track government spending. He also helped war veterans.

EARLY WRITING

Obama's **autobiography** was published in 1995. It is called *Dreams from My Father*. It tells the story of his early life.

CHAPTER 4

OUR
President

Obama told everyone his plan to run for president in 2007. He ran against Republican John McCain. Obama won.

He got to work right away. Many people didn't have jobs. The country was in a **recession**. One reason was because banks gave out too many **loans**. People could not pay the banks back. Obama worked to fix this. He made new rules for the banks. This helped keep people's money safe.

Obama traveled the country to explain why people should vote for him to be president.

MAKING CHANGES

Obama also wanted to fix health care. He wanted every American to have health care. So he signed the Affordable Care Act. It made getting health care easier for most people.

Obama won a second **term** in 2012. He pushed for more gun control. He protected **immigrant** children. He stopped them from being kicked out of the country. He also worked to help the environment.

As president, Obama signed many bills into laws.

Obama stood up for marriage equality. He was the first president to do so. The U.S. Supreme Court made same-sex marriage legal in 2016. Now all gay people can get married.

The White House lit up with rainbow colors to show support for marriage equality in 2016.

Obama helped many people as president. His second term ended in 2016.

PERSON OF THE YEAR

Time magazine named Obama "Person of the Year" in 2008 and 2012.

CHAPTER 5

AFTER THE
Presidency

Obama traveled after his presidency was over. He spent time with his family. He rested.

Soon Obama started working again. He wrote a new book. He gave many speeches. Obama wanted to help people in Chicago. He gave $2 million for job training programs in 2017.

Obama continued to give speeches after his presidency.

Obama revealed the plans for his presidential library in May 2017.

Obama also started the Obama Presidential Center. It will be in Chicago. The center will have a museum and library. It will also have a lot of open space with plants. It will open in 2020.

Obama still cares about Americans. He will continue to help make his country a better place for all.

GLOSSARY

autobiography
a history of a person's life written by that person

immigrant
a person who leaves one country to live permanently in another one

loan
money that is borrowed and expected to be paid back

recession
a period of time when a country is not doing well financially

senator
a member of a group of citizens who have lawmaking roles in government

term
a fixed period of time something is supposed to last, such as a position in public office

CHANGE
WE NEED
WWW.BARACKOBAMA.COM

TIMELINE

1961: Barack Obama is born.

1992: Obama marries Michelle Robinson.

1996: Obama becomes an Illinois senator.

2004: Obama is elected to the United States Senate.

2009: Obama becomes the first African-American president.

2012: Obama is elected for his second term as president.

ACTIVITY

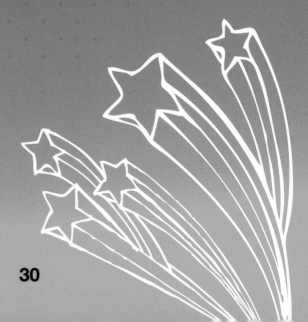

MAKE A LAW

What laws would you make if you were president? Choose a cause that is important to you. Research your cause. Make a plan for how your law would work. Then teach others about it. Present your law to the class. Encourage them to support your law. Then take a vote on how many people support your law.

FURTHER RESOURCES

Want to read more about the Obamas?
Learn more with these books:

Doak, Robin. *Michelle Obama*. Extraordinary Women. Chicago: Capstone Raintree, 2014.

Souza, Pete. *Dream Big Dreams: Photographs from Barack Obama's Inspiring and Historic Presidency.* New York: Little, Brown and Co., 2017.

Interested in the government?
Check out these websites:

Ben's Guide: Federal Versus State Government
https://bensguide.gpo.gov/apprentice-federal-versus-state-government

National Geographic Kids: Presidential Fun Facts
https://kids.nationalgeographic.com/explore/history/presidential-fun-facts

INDEX